Signature Book Printing, www.sbpbooks.com

www.howtheskunklearnedtojump.com

www.cedarspress.com

_____

ISBN 978-0-9820033-0-5

Library of Congress Cataloging-in-Publication Data

Schumann, Stephen and Penni

   How the Skunk Learned to Jump / Schumann Stephen : Schumann, Penni

48p. cm.

Summary: Five year old boy learns that he is determined be an Olympic Nordic ski jumper.

HOW THE SKUNK LEARNED TO JUMP

Written By

Stephen Schumann and Penni Schumann

Illustrated By
Penni Schumann

Cedars Press, LLC

Dedicated to my family.
Thanks for all of your support
(especially Dad for driving up the canyon).

Ski Jumping is fun.
Taking off with speed,
Sailing through the air
Like a bald eagle.

By Stephen Schumann

February 2008

In the summer of 2005, when Stephen and his dad went to the Utah Olympic Park in Park City, Utah, Stephen discovered what he wanted to be when he grew up....

As they turned up the road to go toward the Olympic Park, Stephen said, "Wow! Dad, what are those two big green hills with lines on them?"

"Those are the Nordic ski jumps. Look! There goes a jumper. Did you see him?" said his dad.

"Awesome! Can I do that?" he asked as he gazed out the window searching for more jumpers as they drove up the winding hill with the jumps coming into view and disappearing with the tight turns in the road. Each time Stephen saw the jumps he eagerly said "There's one!"

"No, Stephen you're only five. Jumping is for big boys. We are here to see the bobsled track, those Nordic jumps, and learn about the winter sports in the 2002 Olympics. You don't remember them because you were only two.

"Now this park is also used for training athletes in bobsled, skeleton, and the luge, which are all sliding sports. It is also used to train athletes in aerial jumping, which is when the athletes do flips and twists in the air before they land, and Nordic jumping, which you just saw." his dad added.

They finally arrived at the top of the mountain. Stephen looked down at the road. Looking around he saw the aerial jumps, a swimming pool, and the bobsled run. In front of him was a large glass building, which was the museum and their first stop. In the museum, Stephen learned what each of the winter sports is about. He was able to sit in a bobsled, lie down on the luge, try virtual downhill racing, and stand next to the really huge bison puppet used in the Olympics' Opening Ceremony.

As they exited the museum, they heard a huge splash. "What was that, Dad?" Stephen shouted as he ran toward the aerial jumps and splashing sounds.

Stephen's dad explained, "This is training for the aerial ski jumpers. The athletes go down that ramp and do a jump and twist or somersault and land in that big pool. The water protects them from getting hurt. It is a soft landing. After they have learned their jump, then in the winter they can learn to go down a snowy ramp and land on the snow." Kids of all ages were walking up the steep stairs to go down the ramp again and again into the pool. Stephen jumped and clapped as he watched athletes go down the ramp, soar high into the air, and then splash into the pool.

After a while they walked over to the bottom of the bobsled track, where there is now training for the luge, skeleton, and bobsledding events. The sky was a deep blue, and the mountain breeze helped cool them under the hot summer's sun. They hiked up the hill on the snake like winding path that ran alongside the track to the top of the bobsled run.

From the top of the hill they could see across the valley. As they caught their breath from the climb, Stephen heard someone say, "Hey, kid, do you want to see us go off the big jump?"

"Yes," Stephen shouted. As he ran toward the boy with long skis who had called to him, he yelled back toward his dad, "May I? Please, Dad!"

The boy invited Stephen and his dad into the building that has the platform where the jumpers start. He said, "Come in here so you can see us jump really well."

They went into the building and stood right at the top of the largest Nordic jump, 120 meters long, and gazed downward to the bottom of the hill. "Wow, look how far down that goes. The people look so small!" Stephen said in amazement.

They were captivated. Stephen stood still, practically holding his breath and studying the boys' every move as they laid down the skis, stepped into their bindings, and fastened the skis to their boots. Then they sat on a bar at the top of the jump, and turned their legs and the skis to point down the hill. When they were ready, they stood up off the bar, went straight down, and jumped the largest Nordic jump. He heard the hum of the long skis going down the plastic track until the athletes jump at the end with a grunt and a whoosh.

"Wow!" exclaimed Stephen, gazing down the long hill as he watched each boy jump. "Dad, they look like they are flying."

They stayed at the top talking to the jumpers who told them they were here from Canada training. The Canadian boys told them that the beginning of the jump where the athletes gather speed before they jump into the air is called the "in-run." The in-run for the 120 -meter jump is about as long as a football field. The Nordic jumps in the Olympics are 90 and 120 meters.

When Stephen's dad said, "We really have to go now." Stephen begged his dad, "May, we go watch them from the bottom and see them land better, please?"

They caught the ski lift down and watched from the bottom until the jumping ended. As they walked up the hill back to the museum parking lot, Stephen said, "Dad, I want to do that. I want to ski jump."

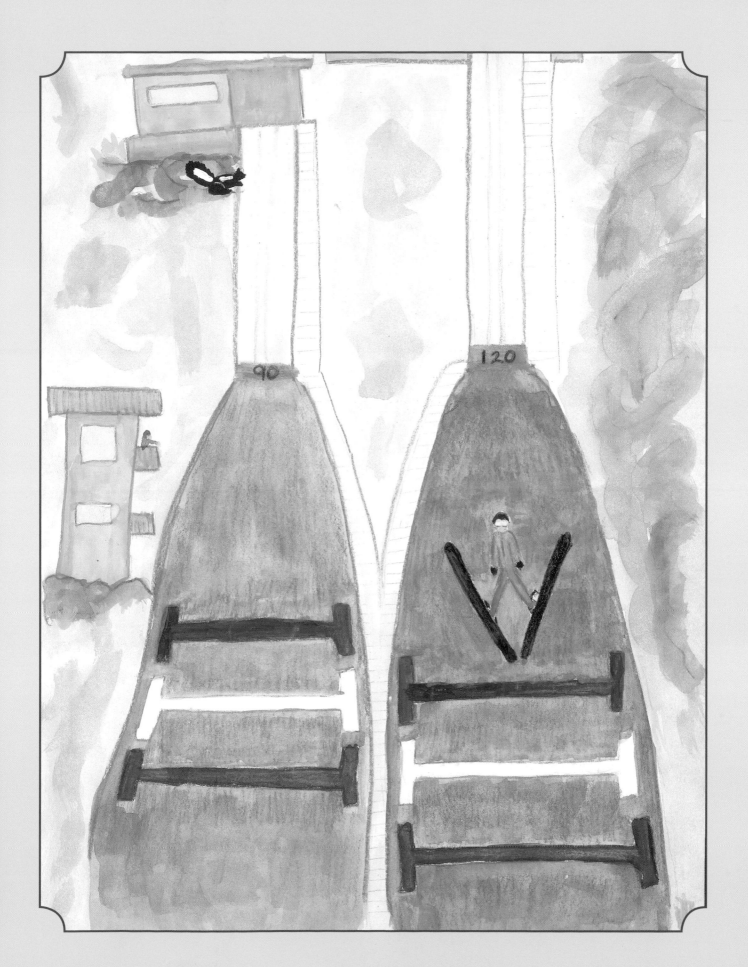

When he got home, Stephen's mom asked, "How was the Olympic Park?"

"It was great. Mom, I really want to ski jump," Stephen said very seriously.

"That's nice, Stephen, but you are only five. When you get older we will look into it," replied his mom.

Stephen was so disappointed. He needed his parents to understand that he really wanted to learn to jump and fly like those boys from Canada. Stephen didn't think he was too young, so he decided to beg, "Mom, I want to ski jump!" "Please, please, please let me learn to ski jump!" He asked his mom and dad over and over and over again.

Finally, after six or seven months of listening to Stephen's begging, his dad called the Olympic Park to find out if there were even lessons for children as young as five. He was surprised to learn that usually the coaches like the kids to be about seven years old. Although Stephen was only five, because he could alpine ski, the coaches invited him to attend a 'learn to fly' camp.

"Yeah! I get to jump! Three mo-ore days until the camp starts. Thre-e-e da-ays. Mom, I told you I could learn to fly," shouted an excited Stephen as he jumped around his mom's kitchen. Stephen was so excited he could hardly wait for three days to pass. Every morning for the next three days Stephen woke up at 5:30 am saying, "Is today my learn to fly camp?"

At the first lesson the kids were given nicknames by the coach. Stephen became "Skunk," because he had a helmet cover with a white tail on it. He wasn't sure about being called a Skunk, because he didn't want the other kids to think he was stinky and say 'pee-u' when they saw him. But he decided it was all right when he heard the other kids had funny nicknames too: Giggles, Pacman, Corndog, Party Boy and Skizil. Whether Stephen really liked it or not, the nickname stuck, and everyone on the jump hill called him Skunk.

After getting his jumping name, Skunk was told by the coaches to hike up the hill a little way, put on his alpine skis, point the skis down the hill, and swoosh, go straight down the hill without turning, jump over a little bump, land, and eventually stop on the flat part. "Phew! I did it," he whooped when he reached the bottom.

When that got easy and Skunk could land without falling every time, the coaches invited him to go up higher and make the in-run longer. After about the third lesson and he could do a seven meter jump without falling, his coaches said, "Skunk, let's get you on jump skis." Skunk was given real Nordic ski jumping skis, which were longer and wider than his alpine skis.

Skunk's dad, who was nearby watching, heard him say, "Hey, Dad, these skis are as tall as you." He looked up at the top of the skis and tried to reach the tips with his hands.

Skunk discovered the ski jumping boots were also different from his alpine boots. The boots laced up and were not as heavy and stiff. He also learned that only the top part of the boot is attached to the ski. So when Skunk first put on the skis, he struggled and fell, often tripping over the long skis, which were hard to muscle around. "Ugh!" But after practicing on those huge skis at home on the grass, he got used to them.

When Skunk took his super long jump skis back to the jump hill for his fourth lesson his coaches told him to hike up the hill like the first day: hike up the hill a little way, put on your skis, and go straight down!!

Oops! Thud. He fell. Skunk found the jump skis hard to control. But after a while on the jump skis and no falls, he was moved to the five meter jump. Yeah!

Jumpers learn early that form is very important. They have to jump out over their skis. To help the beginning jumpers learn this, the coaches ask them to practice the "imo," which is short for imitation jumps. Skunk loved learning imos and practiced them whenever he had a chance.

"Mom, Watch! I need to stand with my feet together, bend my knees, and hold my arms straight behind me. This is how I hold my body in the beginning of the jump on the in-run before I fly into my coach's hands with a straight body, just like Superman," said Skunk. "If I get all squiggly or soft, then I will tip in, which means I will fall and hurt myself," he added. Stephen loved imos and practiced them at home all the time: on his bed, on the sofa, and on every chair saying "Catch me!"

Skunk learned quickly to always listen to his coaches because good form is safe. And better yet, if he pays attention to the coaches and has good form they let him jump the bigger hills.

It took lots of practice on the five meter jump on jumping skis and lots of imo practices. He tried and tried not to fall when he landed, but it was really hard. "Skunk, don't forget to set your ankles and straighten your legs," reminded his coaches.

Finally after many tries he landed. "Yeah! Skunk!" yelled all the coaches and the people watching. He loved hearing the cheers. His mom and dad loved seeing Stephen's smile.

Pretty soon he was landing well, and he asked his coaches "May I move to the ten meter jump?" On the last day of the season, Skunk jumped the ten meter and landed it!

At the end of the winter season during the club's award ceremony, Stephen was awarded 26th place overall. He was not discouraged. His only comment about the night was, "Mom, did you see Anders Johnson? He was just in the winter Olympics in Torino, Italy. He is so sick." Stephen learned that being 'sick' is very cool in the jump world.

Stephen and his family quickly learned that the jumping community is fabulously supportive of each other regardless of their age and ability. Often they will see the older kids who jump the big hills standing on the side of the small hills with the coaches.

Even though ski jumping is a winter skiing event there is still practice during the summer. In the summer the in-run for the jump is all plastic, and the landing hill is also plastic like a broom or a carpet with long plastic straws, which get watered down with sprinklers to make them slippery.

Skunk loved ski jumping. So he continued with lessons in the summer. His mom and dad got him a special ski jumping suit and a new ski jumping helmet (which had to be painted with a white stripe down the middle to match his jump name.)

To get to the top of the hill, Skunk still has to take the skis off and carry them up the hill. Jumping on the plastic was like starting all over again. On his first try, he fell with a thud and slid to the bottom. "Ouch!" But as all the other jumpers, he kept standing up, and hiking back up the hill to do it again. After about one month, Skunk got used to the plastic. Not only was he jumping the ten meter jump, but he was jumping so well that he was invited to go to Canada to train and enter a competition. Skunk was so excited. "Dad, I get to go to Canada! The place where those boys were from, whom we met last summer."

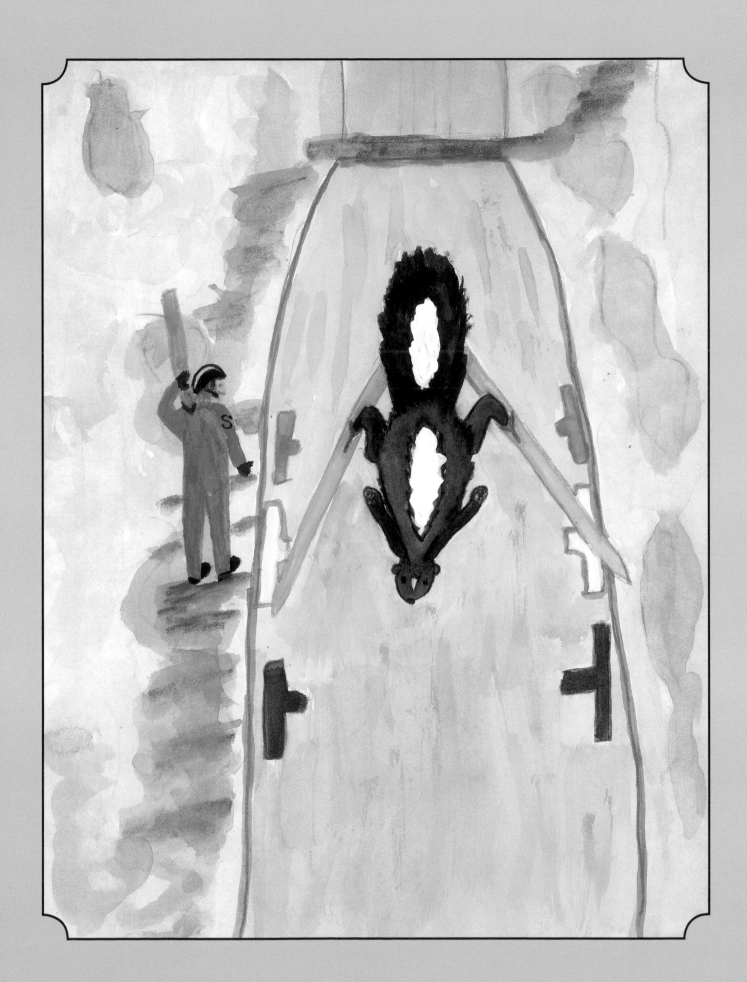

So the Skunk, his coaches, and his dad went to Calgary, Canada to compete. When he was there, he met yet another Olympian, "Slick," a ski jumper with the Canadian National Ski Team. Slick helped coach Skunk and the other young jumpers. But Skunk liked most that he just hung out with them. While in Canada, Skunk entered his first Nordic Combined event. He had to run a kilometer and Slick ran alongside him for the whole distance. As for the jumping, Skunk did well and was awarded third place.

When Skunk got home his mom asked him, "How was the trip? Did you have fun?"

Skunk answered, "Mom, I want to be an Olympic ski jumper. I know that it will take lots of practice, but I want it more than anything in the world. It will be my biggest dream come true."

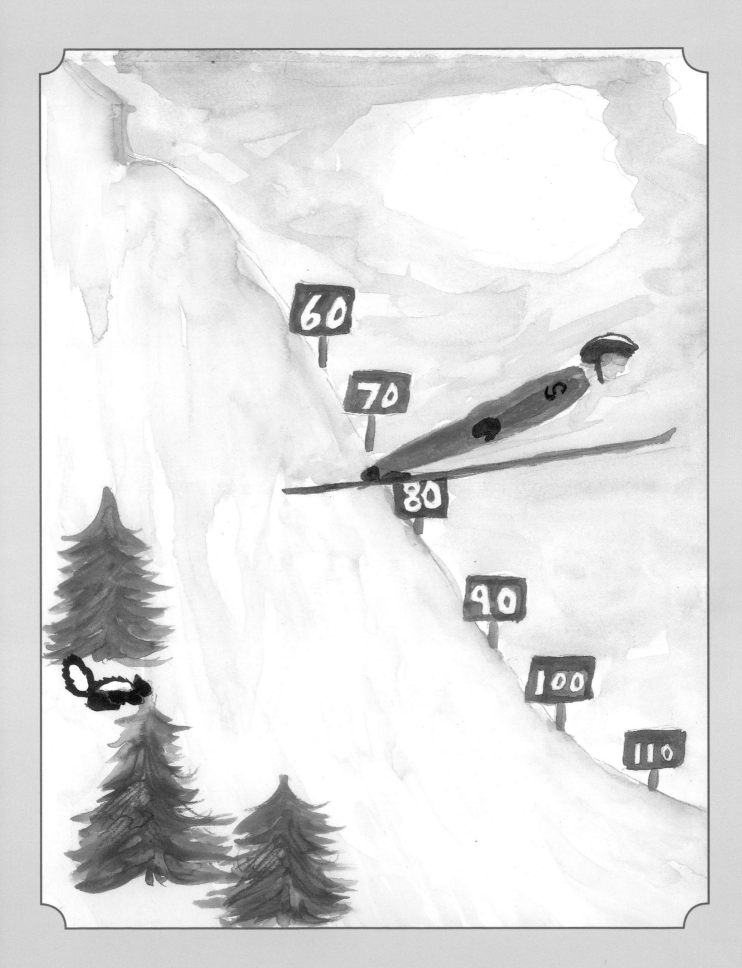

First year jumping

Skunk in Calgary on the 38 meter jump

Stephen the Skunk